Hawksley Workman

hawksley burns for isadora

With paintings by Beverley Hawksley

Gutter Press

Copyright © 2000 Hawksley Workman

All rights reserved. No part of this book may be reproduced or transmitted in any form or by any means – graphic, electronic or mechanical – without the prior written permission of the publisher.

The publisher gratefully acknowledges the assistance of The Ontario Arts Council and The Canada Council for the Arts.

Canadian Cataloguing in Publication Data
Workman, Hawksley, 1975-
Hawksley burns for Isadora
Poems.
ISBN 1-896356-35-4
I. Title.
PS8595.O68H39 2001   C811'.54   C2001-900329-3
PR9199.3.W67H39 2001

Edited by Anna-Marie Reilly

Published by Gutter Press, P.O. Box 600, Station Q,
Toronto, Ontario, Canada M4T 2N4
voice: (416) 822.8708, fax: (416) 822.8709
email: gutter@gutterpress.com

Represented and Distributed in Canada by
Publishers Group West Canada, 250A Carlton St.
Toronto, Ontario, Canada M5L 2L1
Toll Free: 1-800 747.8147   fax: (416) 934.1410

Design...4dT
Paintings by Beverley Hawksley
Manufactured in Canada

Preface

To the playful,

Bless those who arrive on horseback. Bring water and fresh loaves of bread for their pleasure. Bless the bee keeper and the knife sharpener, and hear their earthy blues. Bless those who play like children. May they infect all those who doubt. A knowing wink to you.

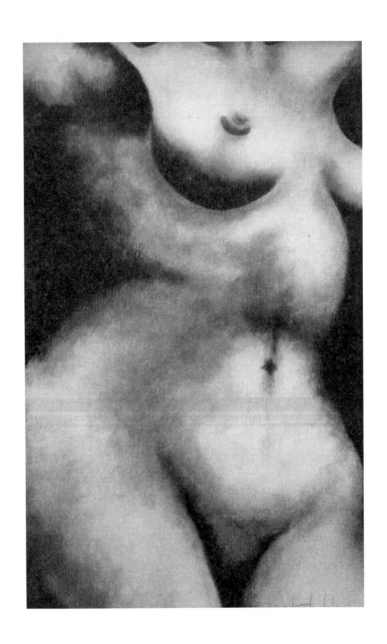

ISADORA,
Funny that you should drag me kicking and screaming to the water. Ye beautiful Isadora of mine eye. Kicking and screaming can look like singing and dancing depending on whether you're watching from an island or a star. "If you're quiet," she softly scolds, "you can hear the shiny bodies sliding from their slippery perches into the Motherworld."

I read that the reckless dreamers were growing gills, Isadora. I think you're on to them; the fire breathers. They're beating at our backs, threatening to melt our waxy feathers down. "Patience," you breathe. "Slowly invite each oxygen molecule from the water into the clumsy rhythms of your lungs." Dust off your memories! Listen to your tiniest cells. They've been waiting to return.

Hawksley

ISADORA,

How can you be so patient with me? I'm speechless before your beauty. I will open wide. Trust that I will open wide enough to drink you into my guts.

How can I be lost in this muck? You've spread your love so fair and true before me. Oh the beauty of the noises you breathe into my ears. The gurgles of newly-born mermaids. Stories of the ancient unions of the moon and ocean. Sweetness, you drip in the fullness of time, selflessly, while I dissolve in careful teaspoons selfishly. Alas, I have been to these shores before, to steal a whiff of that healing, salty breeze. I knelt and left, hunkered away in the shadows. I never cried. "You cannot race in this love. You cannot race where there is no beginning and no end." Isadora, your patience is a blessing.

Hawksley

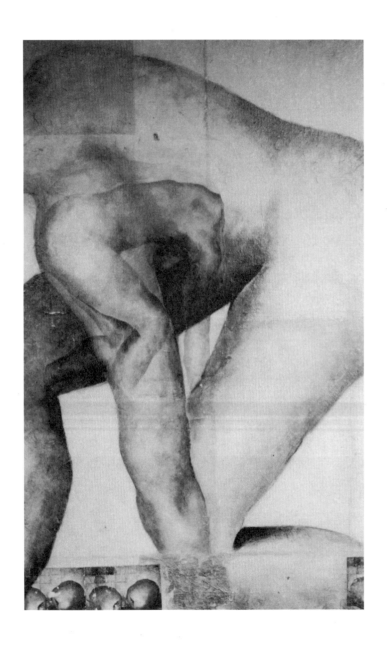

4

ISADORA,
Let us speak of the times we live in now. It is too easy to choke on the beauty of our dreams, to just close our eyes and devour. Let us speak of soldiers in rusty armour. Let us kiss while spider's tongues twist to taste our toes. Let us bathe in dirty water. Let us beat the midnight drums. The ones that summon those lusty animals we forbid ourselves to feed. Let us drill holes in red boats. Let us eat handfuls of sand to grind the walls of our gizzards clean. Let us tear the flag poles down and forget our names. Let's have our organs hanging in the cages of our bellies as we roam on all fours. Let us pull the petals from lovers' roses. Let us eat at earthworm supper tables. Let us slip into jars of nails. All of this, and let us never forget where we came from.
Isadora, I'm your earth-bound candy treat. I'm simple. I'm the one who needs a snorkel to breathe underwater. I'm the one with a wagon-load of shoe polish and peas. I'm all appetite and envy. I'm all for you, strapped by tightly wound ropes to fire and stones. I'm brisk, winter, lemon icicles melting to drop on your tongue. I know the dance moves and destinations but long for the journey with you.
Hawksley

Isadora,
Whoever was forgotten will be remembered. For, wrapped up in wine-stained cloth is a brown berry. An old, weathered, brown berry, sweetened by the truth of its waxing wisdom. Delicious and sacred, like burial honey. This berry is the bargaining jewel in the spiritual dealings of blue bears and white swans. The funny, old relic perches lost songs on the lips of the selfish and forgetful youth, like bells on sleepy kitten's collars, sending them to sing on early-morning street corners. The ears that would never listen, like deafened corn fields, suddenly tune in and quit their work to stomp around muddy fire pits and sing: Kalawa lua lua, labadada lua lua, chaquaqua lua lua. (Moonwater beauty beauty, fire-breather beauty beauty, wise brown berry beauty beauty). Isadora, our voices will never strain when we sing together, the healing hymns of our water-mamas. Our berry juices ooze so freely from sex-charged centres. The places of animal urgency, and puddle purity. The places we live to draw kitchen curtains over steamy panes when our black kettles burn to boil over on each other.
 Oh enough! Hear the straight words woman. I've a thousand dripping candles, all alight and twinkling for you. Let's dust our sweaty foreheads with fragrant ashes and toast to truest love, knowing, that when we light our pasts we see our futures.

Hawksley

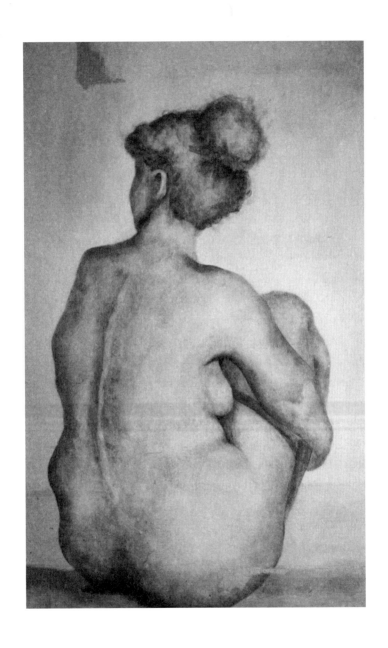

Isadora,

Can we be wooden wheels splintering on this rocky route? We show the wear of distance. We're bleached a bit by sun. And as our stories trickle out by the fires we build, our vessels start to disappear. These dusty blankets serve us well tonight in the cool desert night. Perhaps these grains were whittled painfully from rocks to these finely laid jewels. You never give pain more credit than it's due. You cover your teeth from sand and flies with splendidly dyed scarves. The winds of these plains burn my eyes to tears. You remind me to be careful of the water I waste. For the deep roots of these survivalist nomads, these harbingers of green life gleaned from the utterly impossible; document each drip individually. Each tiny, painful splash in baked mouths, prayed for and celebrated. But look at you woman. You're an ocean on horseback here. You're a cool well where mothers gather to speak of the love of their sons. This infinite hot sand seems more like your inviting shores, your tides to break and grace clumsy beach dwellers. Your breath makes misty life wet enough to dampen the buoyant buzzard's wings. Some fly too close in their nosiness, that their wings get soggy and heavy and they fall from their wanton flight to the the ground. You laugh. You're the only one laughing in the desert. Bless the shed layers of lizards and snakes. May their rebirth continue in the mire of these dry, ashy fields. You jest "Look around you, silly man. Powdered life as far as you can see, just add water."

ISADORA,

Who's making love anymore? Who's churning up homemade ice cream anymore? We used to go into fits of sneezing when we first started making love. You said it was the dust being stirred up from our beautiful bodies. I had dust thick enough to darken my brightest light. Oh that heavy, sleepy dust. Dusty candle sticks. Dusty ballrooms. Dusty fireplaces. Dusty kitchens. If tonight is as dark as last, let's dip ourselves in honey and make sweet ice cream 'til morning light.

Now who puts beauty in a long grey cloak in these times? Who makes beauty into this stranger to be the unknown and feared? Is this the work of the one who hides our beauty under tired blankets of dust, who stiffens our joints, making our bodies and passions brittle? Well, let me say this; there looks as if there might be a good reason to melt the spoons into bullets, to pull together the armour, or better yet, to strip absolutely naked in the face of this fear-maker, and let the truth of our beauty do the talking. 'Cause baby, nothing makes me angrier than when we conceal ourselves out of fear. Beauty itself may not be worth our blood, but the truth of it, sure as blue, is.

Hawksley

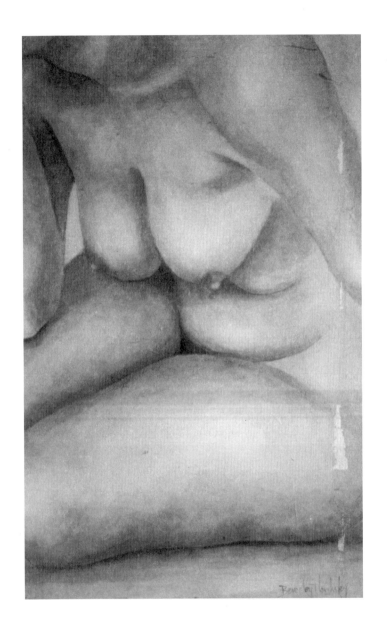

Isadora,
What are these rhythms that infect my hips when I meet you? Hypodermic needles carried by golden beams, filled with animal serum, to land in my thighs. Woe the domesticated animal. See the lineage, monkey-man? The broken human, the pet dog, as man's best friend, and the critical cat (like alien observer), tricking us each moment as we go. The purr that rumbles from the core is wild like the centre of burning planets. Meanwhile the bumbling, graceless panting of the lanky canine seeks specs of patronizing affection to comfort its noon-time nap. Radio waves go to the heavens from magnetic poles. The mother broadcasts her truth on all frequencies. Never for the need of response. For she is no dog. Truth is truth for as far as the eye can see and further. The kitty-cat disappears momentarily to communicate with the mothership, and returns to the table. Message received. Oh the ancient, sex rhythms of moons and motherships to play upon our eardrums. Isadora, you and I can clip our whiskers and close our eyes. Our tongues will never be the wiser. We'll make our love in the breezes of the bushes, and by the light of floating candles.

Hawksley

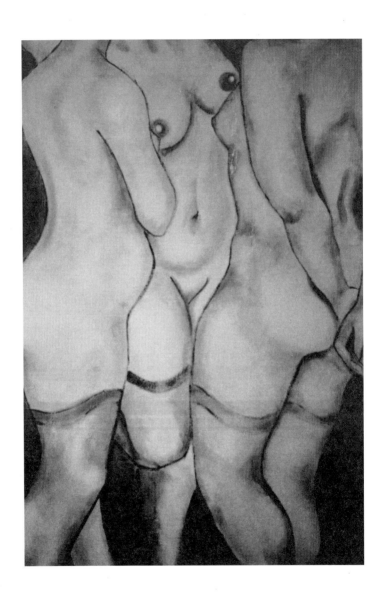

ISADORA,
Last night we were the delicious wolves. Thirsty tongues brought pleasure tides to wash our lusty centres. We rolled naked in hills of shag tobacco till our skin stained autumn yellow. We heard the howling of harvest moons. We felt the healing clean of saliva licked on our wounds. We burned like offerings of summer berries on a ragged forest alter. We spoke fluently in ancient codes of quiet and water noises. Oh the mud. Oh the sweet spoons of malted barley. Oh the seasons. Oh the gatherers of lovers to the grind, keep me walking. Give me oil in my lamp, or if I have no eyes, make me to slither with my ear close to the pulse beneath the peat growth. Remind me with every thistle scrape, my love, with every stubbed toe, of the beauty in the lost art of imperfection.

Hawksley

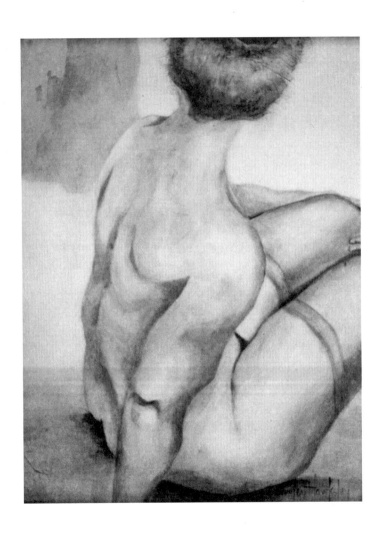

ISADORA,
Distant woman, are you receiving? Are the fringes clear? Have you begged for wisdom as I have? Have you breathed up the smoke signals? Oh, the closed gates and buried keys. You are the merciful hammer to smash the locks, to free the mobs of sad, starving souls. Your prayers are wintergreen. The nay-sayers sail back and forth just within sight of the harbour docks. Their red eyes in telescopes from nosy crow's nests burn holes in the backs of the weak and ill-convicted. You set us down, in full view, to a picnic of bee pollen and twig tea. You don't seem worried or afraid. Our toes dangle in the water. In your love, exists no questions, and hence no need for answers. There is peace in faith. Like giving yourself in full to the flow of seasons. Just as red berries cuddle in early autumn winds. Doubt wears rusty cans around his ankles. He wipes his nose on the red flag he waves. He plants crops of twine-weed in the specks of imperfection (that lie in true beauty) to trip blind lovers.
I hear your prayer. Peaceful smoulder. Warm hands. Soft moves perfected in harvest moon light. A kettle simmers. Dew-drop tongues touch. In brown bellies, there is only this. No questions.

Hawksley

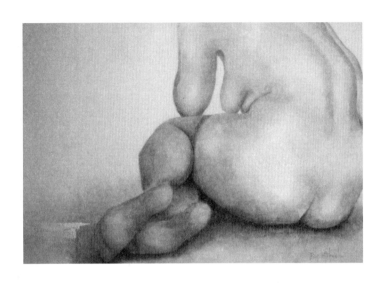

ISADORA,
Undress slowly. Take all night. Suck into the last droplets of fire light. Shake away the crusts for the pigeons. Tattoo a secret on your ankle for the grave robbers. Keep them guessing. Let the dragging road-jaws grind themselves to dust. Slowly, woman. Down to your scent. I'll peak through hedges to see your paradise. It's winter out here, but you melt my frozen tongue with sweet lava-like berry juice. Dry the dinner plates on the clothes line and pot plants in the wine glasses. We'll take steamy horses over frozen rivers carrying our precious cargo of ancient light in deep mirror buckets. Sniff the sleeping gardens. Pluck the blue buds of watery wisdom from the otherworld's deep flow, then tuck the jewels in your cheeks to pass the border guards. Those jagged-tooth nightmare dwellers wear dark heels to squash dreams under foot. Oh sweetness we'll shred our passports into wild bird's wings to spread the horizon. Tonight we'll travel forever in our kiss, never to return here again. So, quiet woman. Drench yourself. Undress slowly. Let this journey last. Arrival is surrender. Let us never arrive.

Hawksley

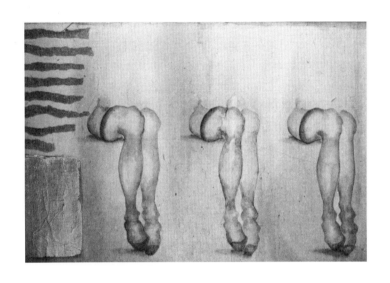

ISADORA,
I painted over the lens of my telescope, locked the observatory door and threw the key into the swan pond. It's time to be here in the dirt and goo. Now, more than ever. I woke up the other afternoon curled up beside a dozing cow in a field. As she slept, I listened to her belly. Two stomachs churned away at daisies and grass harmoniously. Weather balloons snooped on us and reported to the papers and waves that I was suckling a milky moon in green skies. Oh the distance, oh the currents. Oh the tiny cricket singer performing love ballads on burning horizons. Lo, the jangling carts of the traveling winter circus never show on the blistered lips of sun drenched beaches. But I've heard they have white tigers playing xylophones made of tuned icicles. The music they make is alleged to be so beautiful that audiences leave and cut their ears off to never hear another sound as long as they live. And here I say to you (tasting your sweetness with the mud between my toes), burn up my flying papers baby, cut off my tongue and call me... Earth-Boy-Blue. There's no muck or lollipop out there that would be as right and delicious as this.
Hawksley

ISADORA,
You are as bread and fireworks to my nighty-night time insides. You rise and cool on dirty stone bellies. Wispy buffalo migrate like plasmic ghost bodies beneath the heavy cover of black, tear duct clouds. You remember that long walk? You said we'd be back for supper. But we grew old and grey and our bones got brittle as we went. We finally fell completely to dust, and the foxes gathered us in to paper bags and carried us gingerly to where we came from. Our remains were promptly buried beside each other with our cold plates of uneaten dinner. A few rubies showed, and the hidden kernels turned to gold in the husk. Oh, but my belly is stuffed and the dark corners briefly lit. I stand with my hands full at the harbour inhaling the morning mist. Inhaling the mourning missed. Somewhere someone wakes up late from a dream about flying machines, and decides to change their name. I prefer the slow float. The gunpowder burning eyes. The smell of flax bread baking. The decay buried by white snow. Thursday's blue. Lighty-light my insides, sweetness-mine. We'll lay like dust 'til pinky dawn makes our eyes anew.
Hawksley

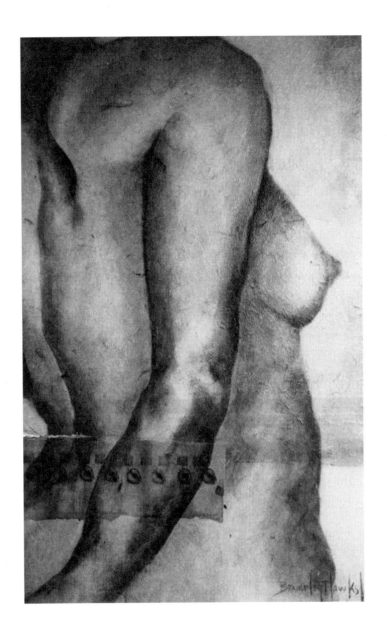

Isadora,
Oh the fine chemicals pounding from our passion glands. The sun-baked bricks that make our cage. Dark, imported spice teas. Fine green fruit picked from trees on hills I've never seen. Oh the decadent flavours of your flow. Rose petals delicately sewn together to make the sheets that cover our bed. Hanging light fixtures filled with bleeding candles swinging in the midnight breeze. Weightless, never waiting. Cold horses snort vapour in tiled stables. The smell of cinnamon escapes from forest floors. Colour birds coo melodies composed in our warmth. Turned soil and pumpkiny shag. Our sexes crush into one another and fires lick our bellies from the inside.
Remember how we hold each other in these autumn nights. Remember the black iron stove. Touch my lips. Sip long and true at this cup. Savour every joy and sorrow. Prop your eyes open with twigs and stare into the light. Join with me baby in a feast of dirt candy. Keep us walking, I pray, for I am ready for anything.
Hawksley

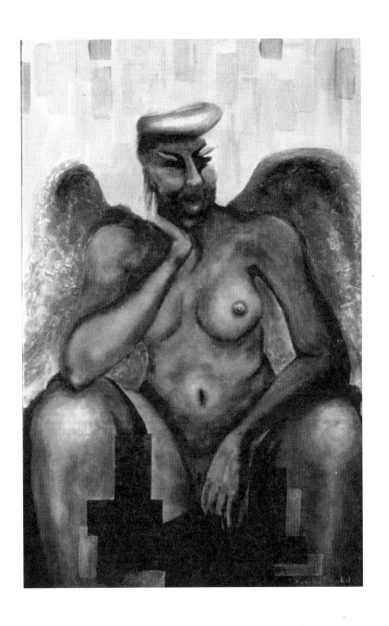

ISADORA,

Have I sacrificed enough? Have I ditched the skin? That gooey layer that never lit. Have I dove down the chimneys with mile-wide nostrils vacuuming the soot? Have I been a painter who chops off horse hairs to stir into the plaster walls? Chew off my finger, and chaw it down. Bottle my body heat to sell to the snow people. No pain, no tears – no reason to be a pretty blister. Sing-a-song-a-supa-supa. Who knows of ancients better than you? Who knows their struggle? You etched each story with a sharpened wooden spoon, carefully, into your elbows and knees. The special secrets you tattooed to your teeth like drawings in a cave. I suppose I could be a boy and be angry that I've kept myself on the end of a fishing string, or I could be a girl and be happy that I dangled above the mist. Sweet silk worms cheeking on my tired voice box. How many layers to painfully shed before I can sing with no pants on? No pants on. No man's land. I'm a scared little mouse waking from dreams of being eaten alive by a wolf. The sounds of my little bones crunching should not deter me. Woman, you help me love the fear. It keeps me moving and wise. Three kisses to you, fair, strong woman of the fair.

Hawksley

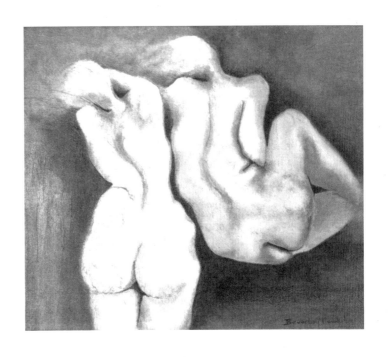

ISADORA,
Truest true. I break down to sand just to be at your feet. Bleach me to sunny snow just to dip me in your soup. Your deep gutsy green scuffed by the feet of the hordes that flock to hear you wail. Quiet tears later. Oh the halls of my heart ring with your songs. They play in my dreams. You move like water. Fill me. I am a wooden bucket. Drip on me. I am a stone. Cover me. I am a fish. Oh you beauty, I am a spec in the swirl, spinning in the midst of what never started and never finished. Reflecting the light that falls. Woman, we are lovers' eyes open. Breathe into me the burning. Breathe into me. Eyes open.
Hawksley

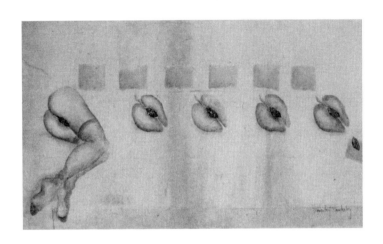

ISADORA,
My jaws ache to bite into you. You peach. You delicious. How deep you tattoo your teeth in to my naked flesh. Animal blood rings in ears like crudely carved stone bells. Clanging. Waking the wolves. Waking the domestic daddy's children from nightmare's of cracking white shells and glaring light. Of being born a turtle baby with a soft shield. We set candles to bathe our faces, to dry the misty lichens that cover our bed where we love. Our limbs tangle with no want of mercy. No want of anything but this perfect meeting of bodies and gnashing teeth. Slow and fast. I see us clinging to breath as we trudge through ice wind over frozen, empty tundra. Desperately, our eyes are watery moons. We're expressionless, our tails don't even wag. There's a time to follow love and be its servant. That's every time. Quiet now, as the mice chitter. Even they hold the tiny heat. You give me every reason to hold steady on this journey, every reason to lay awake to file my incisors sharp.

Hawksley

Isadora,
I've seen the other shades. I've seen where they meet. Twenty. Fifty-six. The donkey was slow. Maybe blind. But the baby was born. Sweet woman, our bodies crash into one another. The collision sounds ring towards distant little forevers. Bouncing off planet faces, burrowing in ant hills. Shine on me when you dream-breathe. The breeze blows into your tender loins. You growl. You tear the curtains from the windows to fashion a wedding dress. It may be midnight, but we will be married. We'll re-marry every night for a thousand years or more, just as we've done so many nights 'til now. We leap. We are like ice cube boots walking a red ember trail. Close your eyes now. Bring your body close. Winter will never outrun us, even as we sleep. The songs of prayer lodge in our mouths. Let us sing through the snow. At the dinner table. On the roof top where we dance. May these sounds heal our ears and those distant ears that hear.
       Hawksley

ISADORA,

The quiet of this night is yours. So listen. Our language has no sound. It's pure. The city looks beautiful at this hour. I see you and I. We're on horses. Riding dead streets. Tall horses. We bump our heads on the stars. But tonight we sleep apart. Tomorrow too. My bed sheets echo like empty rooms. I know you dream. We meet there when we can. But sometimes those pathways come so cluttered. I hear your stirring. You're a broom. I'm dust. You gather. I trust. I've studied your body while you sleep. There's so much more to know. Please be here. I miss you.

Hawksley

Isadora,
Pass this one onto the trusty pilot.
Dry feels dry. In the corner of my eye. I dress like a sequined dolphin to fit the charge. Learn the prettiest words. Creation pain. Ah, but the suffer gives us something to make pictures of. So what you. So what me. So what all these other green blips. We're wired up to feel the supply. So don't short me. No dip. No conductor. Follow? Seek the charms in rotten dogs. Comb out your own bugs. Eat them. Eat hers. Simple things are just as they seem. Soft things too. I hide in my lover sweet. I kiss feet. I stir wax and feathers, but I do it in the dark. I try them below clouds. I walk slow when I'm fat. Like winter. I blast my trumpet in your face when you're cold. Like winter. I trust your parade and the songs you say. Like winter.

Hawksley

Isadora,

Pass this one on to birdie.

What I wears. What I dips myself in. Means nothing. But you guessed all. Knew all. Oh, before I forget, thank you for not nothing. Lovely hand-weaved, berry stained costumes. I see captains and their dresses. Will we wear rings? Ladybugs etching sweet not nothings on the band. Kisses here, kisses there. Kisses flying through the air. Kiss me now, kiss me where. Kiss me when you cut my hair. Oh, your feather fine, your beauty mine. Not for keeps, but in the deeps. I hear all you whisper. Oh you on the ground. Oh me in the sky. Tug my string, I am your kite. Tug my string on through the night. And when the wind fails to make, maybe then we'll take a break. Hear this. The big machines terrify me. Sweetness. You I trust, and I'll fall asleep at your feet. Wake me up when you land this thing.

Hawksley

Isadora,
This one is for the captain.
Captain. Captain. You were such a charm. And old elephant ears, you were a smash. As always, pretty blue left everyone wanting more. Triple blessings to Jimmy Sneezer for blowing the whole thing out. No one thought the dust would ever uncover. But really. The most beautiful of all. The sweet of sweet. The fleshy peach of peaches. With watery moves so soaking, it took a century to mop up the dance floor. Rainy Sunday, or drooling admirers? Oh the mer of maids. The honey bee is too shy to buzz. Isadora. She has my heart. She's a beast. She's a breeze.
Hawksley

Isadora,
Pass this to Pinky. Where the flowers go covered by this blanket of snow. Where we run to, breathless, lovers in an ending time. Where the tears drain in to a weary water table. Where coal fires dwindle by dawn. Where wolves wish well to waning moons. Where lit turnings make their fold. Where sleds stop and dog's steamy noses rest. Where the centuries are in a parade of moments. Where the flags are torn. Where ripe berries fall asleep. Where cups come filled to bury their secrets. Where I meet my delicious. My lover. My strong armed fighter. Where our swords never go. Our swords never go.

Hawksley

ISADORA,
Pass this one to the breeze, and keep a kiss. This one is just for you. My lover. My peace. My underwater breath. My green. My blue. We are moss on rocks. Like turtle babies sunning on their mama's back. The heat is ours. The lucky. The Lovely. Kiss me forever, now. Even as this moment drifts towards its own tiny thimble-size grave, laid to rest beside all the other seconds passed. We celebrate. We move slow. We eat and drink each other. We sing. We scream. We pour. Bulbs flower. Skies dote on our bodies, clumsy and beautiful. We gaze. We know, we don't know.
Hawksley

ISADORA,

You don't end. That's what I like. I've been training my muscles, my organs, my skin, my hair – to last forever. People are ugly. I'll try to be different for you. I'll drag myself through the dark, so you won't have to see. Meeting you in the dark would be best. You twinkle by moonlight. That's what I dream of you. And forbidden things too. I wake. You're never there. I'm never (really) there. I'm back with you. How is it that the day brings light with it every time it comes? Is it not too heavy a burden sometimes? Day could at least spare me the light and just bring us closer. Day is perfect. It's had practice. I like the dark. I know what ugly is, and the dark takes it away. When you're born and dead as many times as day, you know the tricks that make it easy. But you sweetness, are what I'm training for. You don't end. That's what I like. Your beauty isn't your longevity. You never end because your beauty blinds the killer. The killer looks through bellies. He sees everyone's end, but not yours. He works at night. Your light is blinding. Eyes adjust. Mine do. The killer couldn't adjust to you. Most times I don't mind the killer. He's dry and thin. "Did I find bones in the hill? Or is this a hill of bones?" I hear him ask. He pretends to beg, which is just a courtesy. You extend no courtesies. You haven't the time, even as you never end.

Your beauty is uncompromising. So I say a picnic is in order. At the shore. YOU- beauty, the killer and me. We'll await a rainy afternoon, lest the killer will have to shade his eyes. The killer will see into my belly and sigh…"You need to train harder". You won't see me through the sheets I'm wrapped in. The killer will see you through squinty eyes, and fall in love. We always love what we cannot have. I love you most. Because I can't have you most. The killer brings fleshy peaches, that drool in your bite. You bring new rose petals and oil. I bring a basket to carry what's left over. We don't speak. Just the gulls cry. Finally you swim away. The killer speaks "Carry me home, you need the training". "Leave me the basket, I'll eat what's left on the way. I am never full". The whole way he speaks of your beauty. After a ways he says "Drop me here and go on, I have work to do".

Hawksley

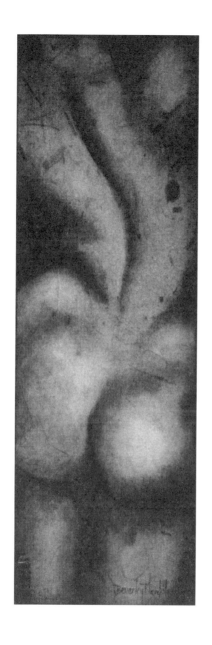

ISADORA,
I thank the bees for the candles and the honey. The bee's stinger is as the Rose's thorn. The rose is more perfect because it is quieter. Silence is perfection. Stones are the most perfect. I am training to be a stone. Making my heartbeat quieter. Tying towels to my feet (to walk quieter). stones don't walk. They're so perfect they've nowhere to go. No desires or wishes. No needs or hunger. Even as I pick a stone up from the ground and carry it with me to learn its secrets, it doesn't object. It's as perfect in my pocket as in the dirt. Perfect in pile or at the bottom of the sea. When I sleep I must most resemble a stone. And when I am a stone I am with you in my dreams. Maybe stones always dream. How did the stone train to last forever? To be so perfectly quiet? Maybe it worked so hard it became eternally exhausted. Left to dream while bees and roses meet. Stones make the killer cry. Everytime I ask, HE WEEPS "Such beauty". You must love the stones as they are. I must change form what I am to have your love. You must love what the killer casts away. All that is perfect and quiet is yours. Everything else is the killer's to end when he sees fit. I want to be yours. I like the killer fine. For picnics now and then and for his wisdom on such things as stones. But I'm training to be yours. Every moment changing from what I am, into what you would have me be. You

sleep underwater with the stones, making love in your perfect ways. I wish to be your favourite stone. So quiet I'm not there. A lover so dear, you would abandon all else. A quiet so quiet that you have never heard. Such quiet it could lull a clumsy, ugly world to sleep in its arms.

Hawksley

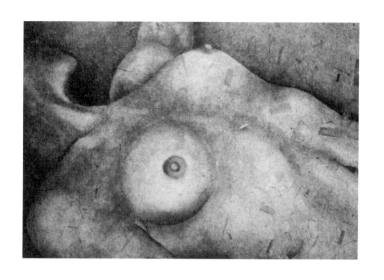

Isadora,

The training is painful. Most painful is the failing. Failing is an ending in its own way. It's a pity. A courtesy, extended to those whose end is their only certainty. I train in the dark, so I can't see my failure. So you can't see my failure. If you knew my failures, you'd never believe me when my training had finally come true. The killer sees my failures. He sees best in the dark. "I see into your belly. Your dinner is singing like a chorus of lonely night toads. Loud and out of tune". Songs are sung. Singing needs breathing. And these silly things run out of breath. I will change to suit you, sweetness. I am sure I too will laugh silently at the night toad's song.

Hawksley

ABOUT THE ARTIST

Beverley Hawksley is a multi media artist living in Muskoka. Her work explores stillness and movement, building layers of thoughts and experiences that make up the ordinary and extraordinary... giving substance to time.